OSCAR AND I

Confessions of a Minor Poet

Peter Phillips

Ward Wood Publishing

Published by Ward Wood Publishing
6 The Drive
Golders Green
London NW11 9SR
www.wardwoodpublishing.co.uk

The right of Peter Phillips to be identified as author of this work
has been asserted by him in accordance with the Copyright,
Designs and Patent Act, 1988.
Copyright © 2013 Peter Phillips
ISBN: 978-1-908742-01-8

British Library Cataloguing in Publication Data. A CIP record
for this book can be obtained from the British Library.

Designed and typeset in Palatino Linotype by
Ward Wood Publishing.

Cover design by Mike Fortune-Wood
Artwork: Mixed Breed Large Scruffy Dog Laying Down
by Adogslifephoto
Supplied by agency: Dreamstime

Printed and bound in Great Britain by
Imprint Digital, Seychelles Farm,
Upton Pyne, Exeter, Devon EX5 5HY

*In Memory of Linda Phillips
and for my family*

Contents

Acknowledgements

About the Author

Acknowledgements

Some of these poems, or versions of them, appeared in:

Acumen, Brittle Star, Frogmore Papers, London Grip, N2 Poetry, Orbis International, Other Poetry, Sofia, South Bank Poetry, The Author, The Spectator, Westminster Review, Weyfarers.

Thanks to my editor Adele Ward, and to Patricia and William Oxley of Acumen, without whose encouragement George Meadows and Oscar would not be drinking and barking their way round the poetry scene.

Thanks also to Mike Fortune-Wood for the quirky cover design.

I want to mention with gratitude my friend and poetry pal, Ian Purser, for his often raised eyebrow, pitying laugh and patience at The George Public House, Wanstead.

OSCAR AND I

Confessions of a Minor Poet

Frank Introduces George

George is often placed or shortlisted – the National,
TS Eliot, Costa – but hasn't won a big one, always

simmers, just below brewing point. He feels poetry
shouldn't be elevated too high. It's the only thing

he never worries about, is still a self-confessed
half-empty man, can down a pint in one flourish

but prefers to be polite and do it in two. He doesn't
mind if his shirt cuffs are frayed, never says no

to chicken Madras, four poppadoms and a Cobra.
Computers make him anxious. He's waiting for voice

recognition, says he doesn't know the difference between
gigabyte or love bite, broadband or brass band.

Those who first meet him probably take his reserve
as standoffish, but he's funny, loyal, and sometimes

disgraceful. When told I wanted to write a piece on him
he said 'Just something short and alcoholic,

a fourteen-liner will do.' I've gone over a bit.

George and Mary at Home

George's landlord wants to buy him out,
needs a tenant with money,
but a rent controlled flat suits George.

He puffs to their fourth floor roof slopes,
its tree top views. Give up their home? Who for?
Some banker boy wanting to impress the Chelsea

girls with his derivatives, turbocharged ego
and his flat. Poetry doesn't sell. Reviewing is patchy,
the youngsters have muscled him away, and teaching?

It would be alright without the students.
Where are the jobs? Who wants an oldie?
He fumbles for the keys.

*

Is that you George?
It is. I could do with some oxygen.
Who else are you expecting? I was hoping...

You were hoping Cyril had phoned.
He expects you at 10am tomorrow, sharp.
Oh great joy! My contract is ready.

I'll clean your shoes, the brown brogues.
I'll wear my giraffe tie. Cyril likes giraffes.
It's only a contract George, why the excitement?

You never know what it might lead to.
Have you got any tinned pears?
We could share them.

It's my turn for the top of the milk.

Signing on the Line

Here we are Cyril, signed
in the right place – not like last time.
I've flicked through and noticed
something about ebooks, no idea
what you mean, but I trust you.

Perhaps you'll be interested when we start
adding the royalties to your cheques.

Oh, does it mean money?

Only if everyone buys the book.

That's your job.

Yes, we'll do our usual stuff, but I'm pleased
you've lined up some appearances at festivals.
You must be getting noticed.

One does one's best.

I see Frank is reading at some of the same events.

We go well together.
I call him a man of letters. He says
I'm a man of postcards.

So you're a comedy act?

Frank's still working on his timing.
I'll see you Cyril, wish me luck.

At a Literary Festival

Sorry we're running late, but I've got time
for two more questions.

Could you tell me where you get your ideas from?

I go to a charity shop, they're usually the cheapest
and I'm helping good causes at the same time.

Are you having a laugh?

That's where most poets go.
The British Heart Foundation and Age UK
are particularly good.
Ah, the lady at the back...
What's your question?

Can you please say what is poetry?

Real poetry is three pints of beer,
followed by a bottle of wine,
preferably one after another,
although you can have a break
of fifteen minutes in between.

That's all. Copies of my book are in the signing tent.
I'm off to the bar.

With the Wine Merchant

Hello Giles, it's me.
What have you got on offer this month?
You know I'm price-conscious.
What is there for a fiver?

We've got an excellent Chilean Merlot
at £4.99, most popular since the miners came up,
and something Spanish at £5.99.

Do you have a bottle open so I can try?

As I've said before, we don't do tastings.

If I take the Chilean
will you allow me a discount?

You could have 10% for a case.

Thank you. Can you deliver?
You know it's not far.

As it's you, when we're next passing.

I don't suppose you could pass this evening?

Battersea Dogs Home

I like the look of that old boy. He seems a bit disreputable.

I wouldn't recommend him, he's not what I'd call a loyal dog.
His name's Oscar. No one wants him.

I'm not looking for a wife. I want a dog for a bit of company.
Where was he found?

At the side of the road in Bloomsbury.

You mean he was in the gutter looking at the stars?

I'm not sure about that.

This is irresistible, too much to have hoped for.
I'll take him. Oscar and I will get on.

Dentist

I only see you with a problem,
you really should visit more regularly,
even if it's just to see the hygienist.

I know, but work gets in the way.

I've never asked what you do.

Er... I'm a writer.

What do you write?

Poetry.

That's interesting.

You really think so?

Absolutely, now lean back.
Open wide. No, wider.
That's better.

The Dinner Party

May I sit next to you, or are you waiting for someone?

Please do, my wife's at the other end.

I've heard you write poetry. What's your real job?

Well... er... yes... I teach a bit.

Are you famous? Should I know you?

There aren't many famous poets these days.

Why's that?

Because there aren't enough readers.

Roger McGough's famous, isn't he?

Yes, that's because he gets on television and radio.

But isn't it because he's funny? I like to laugh.

Would you like to know what I write about?

Sorry, I'm being beckoned. I always go when I'm beckoned.

I can be funny as well... Oh, she's talking to someone else.

George's Poetry Reading

That was a terrific performance –
love the new stuff.
I still don't know how you remember
all your poems. It must be so liberating
not having to look up and down.

It is, but there's a disadvantage.
One has to look at the audience.
I see who's glancing
at their watches and I catch
those wry smiles... and their eyes.

What do they tell you?

Everything. Especially if they're shut.

Being Sold The Big Issue

Are you still here?

I always wait for the last commuters.

It's very cold.
Snow's promised, isn't it?

Who promises snow?
You don't mean commuters?
Do you mean God?

Oh no, certainly not God.
I won't have the magazine today,
here's some change.

Thank you. God bless and before you go,
I'm enjoying the book you lent me,
especially the sad poems.

If it's melancholy you like,
my pal Frank's an expert.
He's a very good wallower.
I'll lend you one of his next time.

With Cyril, his Publisher

I've got some really exciting news –
your poem, Poets on Parade, has been shortlisted
for the Natasha Cambridge Prize.

But I just whipped it off –
I was surprised Vanquished even published it.

I agree it's hard to believe,
and it doesn't stop there.
I've had an enquiry from an American publisher.

But I've been very rude about America.

They don't seem to have noticed.

Perhaps I should try harder?

Not if you want all those dollars
they're throwing at me.

Really? How much?

We'll come to that later. Now do you think
you can behave?

Oh yes, that won't be a problem.
I'll have to practise,
but I'm sure I can manage it.
Now tell me, how much?

With his Wife

Do you still love me?
Of course I do Mary.

Are you sure? Sometimes you seem distant.
It's only the Merlot speaking, or not speaking.

You should drink less.
But it helps – you know.

Don't I help?
You do... you do really.

We're alright, aren't we?
Absolutely.

Let's go out to dinner, to the French.
When were you thinking?

Tonight, would that be ok?
Oh yes, I fancy a nice bottle of claret.

Poetry Class

And you can't use a word like diaphanous.
Yes, it does sound nice...
No, I never said you can't ever use it,

but 'diaphanous dress' is a bit weak,
rather old fashioned, don't you think?
Sort of poetic with a capital 'P'.

It's not really an everyday word –
why not leave it for another poem?
Try 'see-through'. That sounds better.

Please don't raise your voice Pamela,
and I can assure you there is no room
for 'see-through' up my arse.

The Editor of Vanquished

Sybil, thank you for recommending
my sonnet for the Natasha Cambridge Prize.

How could we not? It was masterful.

Was it? I did work on it quite a lot,
for almost a day.

How did you think of the idea –
fusing those images, so evocative of... of...

Everything sort of popped out,
like having a baby.

Oh, you're such a natural poet.
I mean that in the widest sense...
so earth-grounded, you deserve to win.

It would be nice.

You might turn out to be our own Jenny Joseph.
We'd love to make you famous.

The money would come in handy.

There's no money, the trustees award
a hamper from Harrods –
the real prize is winning.

Of course, it would be the greatest
honour; a hamper sounds scrumptious.
Could they include some truffles
and smoked salmon? Hmm, perhaps
I should have spent another day on it.

Oscar Misbehaves

Come on Oscar, it's time you took me for my walk.
Let's go to the Pig and Whistle, the usual
crowd will be there, even that spaniel you like.

Woof.

Don't walk so quickly, you're pulling me along.
Here we are. I'm having a mixed grill and a pint.
What do you want?

Woof woof woof.

You can have my sausage and tomato.
A bowl of water? You are unadventurous.

That was good. Where are we going now?
Home? I still need exercise –
those statins could do with some help. We'll find
a stick and I'll throw it for you.
Would you like that?

Woof.

Right, let's go. Stop that.
Those trousers cost me a packet.
Get down.

Woof woof woof.

Don't you dare swear at me!
You know when I write about this
you're not going to look good.

Arriving at a Literary Festival

Welcome George, thanks for being prompt.
Are you going to read your fish poem? It must
have become quite a curse around your neck.

You mean the one about a trout, or was it a turbot?
I usually try and judge what an audience want,
so if they look like fish lovers, I don't read it.

Surely if they like fish, you would read it?

Oh no. Don't forget, on the surface
the poem's about a grilled turbot,
but underneath it's about sexual behaviour,
so if they are fond of fish as a species,
then I wouldn't want to cause any upset
by grilling a turbot. You understand
I have to be PC these days.

You're so sensitive. Our audience will love you.

Not at all, I always put the punters first;
you never know what oddballs are sitting out there.
We don't want to offend the fish brigade, do we?

Does your Wife Come to your Readings?

I couldn't possibly put her through such misery.

Surely she wouldn't see it like that?

Would you like to hear me read
five or six times a month?

I see what you mean, it might get a bit... boring.

Boring? It can get awfully tedious,
and if I think that, pity the wife.

You make your point most succinctly.

Yes, and she's got to live with me.

With a Student

I wonder if you could read the opening
poems in my first collection?

Sorry dear, but if I read yours
I've got to read everyone's.

But I'm particularly concerned with my 'darlings',
what to do with them.

Keep them. What's the fun
if you can't keep your darlings?

Oh, you really think so?

Absolutely... definitely.

But won't they weaken my work?

They might, but then they might not.

Thank you, you are refreshing.

That's because I've just had three pints.

You don't seem at all drunk.

Good. The Vice-Chancellor told me it's bad form
to be drunk in front of students.
Now, what else can I do for you?

The Problem with Truth

It just gets in the way, Frank. They all seem to feel
because it's true it's got to go in the poem. Imagine

what my poems would be like, if I peddled undiluted
truth. It makes me shiver. Cyril would have a baby,

probably triplets. You should see the quizzical look
on their university faces, when I explain about

sprinkling the essence of truth. You'd think
I was referring to splashing on Brut aftershave.

Dinner with Sybil Archer

So what's this about your funding?

Oh George, you're so good at looking
stern. You seem to have perfected
the art of the frown. Why is that?

Yes, I have three frowns.

Tell me more.

I've got an anxious frown. I use that a lot.
I've got my intellectual frown.
I don't get many opportunities
for that one. And then there's my
quizzical how-to-get-out-of-a-fix frown.

You do seem to be an expert frowner.

Enough of my frowning, Sybil.
Has your funding been withdrawn?

I'll tell you next time, George.

There's going to be a next time?

I hope so. We've been getting
letters about your poems.
I want to interview you for the magazine.
Would you come if I ask you?

I'm sure I could.

With his Grandson

I'm reading poetry for my A levels. Are you a good poet?

What a question! I'm not in the Premier League.

Are you in the Championship?

I'm just hoping not to be relegated.

How do you know your own level?

It's something we sense.
Like knowing you're not strong at maths.

I think you're better than that.

Are you disappointed?

Oh no, the Premier League's alright,
but it's much more fun kicking about in the park.

Thank you, you are a nice boy.
You'll make a good diplomat.

Taking Oscar to the Countryside

Look Oscar, here's a field of sheep. I haven't
written a nature poem for a long time.
Could they be Jersey Royals? Ah, no, they're potatoes.
They seem horribly grubby, not skipping
in the air, just mooching about, heads in the grass.

Perhaps I should describe the sky. Oh, the clouds
look like sheep. That's not good. I can't have
sheep on the ground and in the sky. I'm stuck.
I know, I'll write it down in prose, see what
springs out at me. Come here Oscar.

Don't start chasing, you'll stampede them.
Where did I leave the car? You'd behave
if you belonged to Kevin Crossley-Holland.
You wouldn't dare take advantage
if I had a double-barrelled name.

Talking to his Poetry Pal

Frank, do you think I'm going off the boil?
What did you really think of my last book?

What's brought this on?

Sometimes I feel language is harder to find,
ideas are slippery. Maybe I'm getting old.

I think you're fine.

Fine isn't really enough.
New work has to be better.

You're a bloody good writer.
You can still give those young ones a run
even if you do have to try harder.
Your readings are always sold out,
your books are selling and the festivals
still want you. Just relax.
Show me your new poems.
Shall we have another bottle?

Just what I was thinking.
I feel better already.
Is it your turn?

At a Poetry Tour Boarding House

You were late last night.

The organiser, what's her name,
asked me back for a cup of tea...
No need to raise your eyebrows,
I was a perfect poet.
Do you like tomatoes? Perhaps
I could swap mine for your bacon?

No thanks, I like bacon –
what about my baked beans?
Are you sure you were a good boy?
Have you seen her legs?

Yes, epic, like a racehorse...
I won't have your beans, they tend
to repeat on me.
And I've told you, I was perfect.
But she has got a very nice smile.
Any marmalade?

I've got the last pot, but I wouldn't want
you to feel impoverished. You have it.
I'll have jam.

Thank you. Toast and marmalade will
set me up. Have you seen Frank?
Ah, there you are, Frank. Do you like
tomatoes? I could swap mine for your bacon.

Trying to be Brilliant at a Verse Break Weekend

*George, we want you to come up with a scintillating
strap-line for our new prospectus. Can you do that?*

Sorry Charlotte, I'm not in advertising any more.

But it won't take you long, you're so clever.

I've got a lot on today: one-to-ones
this morning, a tricky tutorial after lunch
which I haven't even prepared –
then I'm struggling to make a quorn and carrot stew
and after that the scribblers are giving their readings.

Oh please, we're desperate.

How desperate?

*What if you didn't have to cook tonight
and I did the washing up?*

Yes, that would do the trick.
When do you want it?
You can have it now. What about
'Make love and poetry –
Take a Verse Break'?

*Ah, that's an interesting thought,
we'll have to think about that.*

Glad to help. You'll give me credit, won't you?

With his Uncle

Are you still scribbling?

Well, yes, I –

It must be a nice hobby.

Actually, my next book will soon be out.

Trouble is, poetry doesn't do much, does it?

Oh, I wouldn't say –

I mean you don't feel much after you've read one.

I think that's a bit –

In fact I probably feel worse.

No, it's not like a vaccination.

The only way you'll get some readers
is if you've aimed it at a low level.

Just because –

And it should have lots of rhymes.

Yes, that's exactly what I've done.
So I expect you'll like it.

Sitting for a Back Cover Photo

Where do you want me to sit?

Perhaps if I put you close to the bookshelf
it would make you look more intellectual.

But I don't want to heighten expectations.

I see what you mean. What about a background
shot of the books, would that suit you?

That's much better.
I like the idea of the reader getting
the message I'm bookish. Thank you.
What a very impressive camera.

It's digital now, does everything except
wipe your bottom. I'll take a dozen
and you can decide.

You'll have to advise me, should I smile?
I usually do.

How about looking a bit pensive, can you do that?

Oh yes, that's my fall-back expression.

Ok let's get on with it.

I'm really looking forward to seeing them –
me looking wise and distinguished.

Don't get too excited, this could be tricky.

In Praise of Rejection

What is it that you like about poets, Frank?
I was emailed this question by a magazine
editor, who was doing a survey. Yes,

I know I don't have email, I gave him Mary's.
She hates that. I did feel like telling him
where to put his survey. He's always so rude

with his rejections, I thought I'd reject him.
But the more I pondered, the more I realised
it was a good question. I mean, we mostly

drink with poets – granted Len the Greengrocer
joins in, and that undertaker bloke Ralph
always has something rakish to say, but it's poets

who we gravitate to or seek out. Maybe poets
have grown so used to rejection,
they've come to expect it. It's promoted a bond

that unites us. In a way, don't you think
it's quite nice to be rejected? Of course,
I've got many more rejection slips than you.

Going for a Job at an
Adult Education College

How many candidates am I competing with?

There are six, plus you.

You're lucky to have a good choice.

I must say I'm pleased to see a proper poet
and a male one.

Yes. I'm certainly male.

Sorry, I shouldn't have made a personal remark.

Not at all, I'm glad you noticed.
Does that mean I've got a good chance?

I like you, and just as important,
our students will take to you.

So have I got the position?

I think I can say you have.
You'd be just in time to take part
in one of our...
out-of-door bonding sessions.

Whatever for? I'm not good at outdoors.

It's paint-balling, you'll enjoy it.

Alright, I'll have a go. But what is ball painting?
It sounds beautifully louche.

At the Library

I wrote making an enquiry about leaving
my papers to the library.

What is your name?

Er... George Meadows...

Ah...

Yes, a few of my fellow poets have made
very fruitful arrangements. My wife thought
I should make an approach.

It takes us time to make rigorous enquiries.

Oh, I'll give you plenty of time.
What do you think you could offer
for forty years of scribble?
The wife's agitating for a tropical cruise.

*Grants for this type of acquisition are strictly
limited, even more so with the cuts we are suffering.*

I quite understand, but can I tell the wife
you'll be in touch?

We haven't decided yet.

But if you want to, you'll be in touch, won't you?

Yes, that's how it works.

Thank you. That's enough to keep the wife happy.
And if she's happy I'm delirious.

Being Interviewed by Sybil Archer

So how important is it for poets to be emotionally
engaged with what they write?

I think you'll find the opposite is true.

Really, how can that make sense?

We don't strive for sense, Sybil, and we certainly
don't want blood on the page, that's very messy.
Yes, I suppose repression is the new cool.

What an answer, our readers will love that.
Repression is the new cool –
that will make a magnificent title.
George, you've made me shiver.

Are you cold, would you like to borrow some gloves?

No, but I feel like kissing you. Would that be alright?

Oh yes.

Love Poem for Sybil Archer

George, I just adore your love poems.
Will you write one for me?

My love poems are normally about food.

That's alright. Just imagine I'm a slice of ham.

I'm not in the mood, I'm not even hungry.
I can never just turn it on when I'm asked.

Please, it would mean so much.

But we're not in love, Sybil.
I've only kissed you a few times
and that's because you asked me.

Why not pretend? I'm sure you could pretend.

It's not going to work.

Just write me a few lines, go on.

Alright, but this has had no thought
and you'll probably hate it.
What about:
Oh Sybil, dear Sybil,
your smile makes me dribble.

That's awful, George. You're definitely vanquished.

Thank you Sybil, as usual you're so discriminating.
That's what makes you a wonderful editor.

George Ponders his Situation

I've learnt to dance,
brain and feet in harmony.
I deserve a fish and chip supper.

I'll ask for a half portion of chips.
I like to feel virtuous.
Sybil was a good kisser, she kissed

as if she was hungry. Perhaps she was.
I think she wanted more, but I can't
write a love poem for Sybil.

Life with Sybil would not be a tap dance,
more like a complicated routine –
me being dragged like an old sack

on *Strictly*, across life's poetry stage.
And what about Mary? I'll tell her
I've treated myself to fish and chips,

I'll stress the half portion of chips
and with a flourish, pull from my coat –
da, daa, a wrapped piece of haddock for her.

At the Italian Cafe

Carlo, why do we always end up reminiscing?

Because we've known each other a long time.

It's more than that, it's our shared experience –
children, grandchildren, you know...
and we've never talked about problems,
so we don't groan when we see each other.

You speak for yourself!

And we both dislike those fast-food boys
who bite chunks out of you.
And where can I go for ham, straight
off the bone and just a little grumble?
Can I have another slice?

With the Editor of Poetry Comment

Now what makes you think you're a good reviewer?

I'm a voracious reader, so I'd have no trouble
trotting out all the reviews you want.

Is that all?

Er... I realise I need to give an honest opinion,
with examples from the poems, and now and again
to add spice, I'd be gratuitously rude. That's what
most magazines want, don't they?

It would be totally unacceptable here.

Why are you touching your nose?
Oh, I understand, wink, wink.
Yes, plenty of rudeness, no extra charge.

*That's quite enough. We could never
sanction such behaviour. We'll let you know.*

Is that shorthand for you'll try me out?

Being Evasive

Did you know your mobile's always turned off?

I certainly hope so.

So what's the point in having one?

None whatsoever.
I told you it's just for me.

But what if I want you.

You phone home and leave a message.
I'm usually in, except when I'm out.

But could I send a text
or even an email – would that be best?

Oh no, that wouldn't get me.
I hate electronica, but take down
this number: 4466 9723.
It might help.

How's that going to help?

It's the serial number of my Olivetti.
And I didn't say it would, I said it might.

George Perfects the Art
of Reading The Guardian

Listen to this Oscar. Did you know I'm a genuine
background artist? That's an 'extra' to you and me.
I was asked to read The Guardian about twenty times.
Naturally, sitting in a pub with a pint in hand

was no hardship. The Director particularly sought me out,
said I looked ideal for the part. They even bought lunch,
asked if I had any special dietary requirements,
was I a vegan or wheat intolerant?

I said I wasn't fussy, liked most fatty food
with a portion of baked beans. Oh yes, I said
I had an elegy to ratatouille; they didn't get that joke.
Then I asked if I could bring you along –

you know, 'man and his dog'. Yes, Oscar, you are a dog.
Just reminding you. No, get down.
I said you were well behaved… I overplayed
your inborn decency, so I apologise, you didn't get

the part. I had to sit with a Cairn terrier called Suzie,
too sweet for me, but you'd have gone for her.
She was all top show.
When the Director called 'Action' she wee'd

a puddle over his Hush Puppies.
I tried not to look smug.

Advice on How not to Give a Reading

I get nervous before a reading, does that matter?

No, it should help concentration; I know,
I find it difficult to observe the 'c' word.

I beg your pardon – the 'c' word?

Yes, concentration.

But you recite your poems from memory.

I do, but I still need to concentrate.

Do you think I should go for speech training?

I don't recommend it. An audience doesn't come
to hear you declaiming your poems,
they want to hear your natural voice
with all its strengths and frailties.

But I've written a long poem.
It needs to be performed dramatically.

You may have a problem, Geoffrey, I find
epics don't go down very well –
and I suggest you wear a different dress.

Being Interviewed to be a Poet at a Major Supermarket

Congratulations on winning first prize.

Actually, I was runner-up.

Oh, I suppose that will do.
As our letter said, we're looking for a poet
to teach poetry and spirituality to our staff
and write about our offerings –
mainly food, but also wine.

Oh, I'd love to write about wine.
That's very spiritual.
I've had quite a lot of experience –
I could do some tastings if you like.
Did you have a branch in mind?

We've earmarked Croydon for a trial.

So I'm going to be a trial?

Yes. We'd allocate one of our convenience stores.

A convenience store?
I don't want to be too bogged down.

If it's a success we'll roll it out nationally.

But I want to be in a hypermarket.
Just because I'm a poet
it doesn't mean I'm not ambitious.

Giving Advice to an Aspiring Poet

Find a poetry pal, someone you trust,
who won't make you feel embarrassed,
is a good critic, and a wonderful gossip.

No, I'm not sure someone of the opposite sex
would be desirable, although they might be.
The point is we often make idiots of ourselves;

we need to be able to do that, to expect
the raised eyebrow and the pitying laugh.
We might be a bit reserved if we felt

we were vulnerable to ridicule. In the end
it's the poem that counts, and the friendship.
No, it doesn't work like that. I'm your tutor

I can't be your poetry pal. No it's not
because you're female and I can assure
you I never have a sexist thought... ever.

Before a Poetry Programme Transmission

I understand you're our leading authority on Sulpicia?

Ah... you mean the lady poet of ancient Rome.

Yes, that's her.

Sorry to disappoint, but I'm not really
an authority on anything.

But... but... our researcher was meant to find an expert... surely...

I told Evangeline I knew of Sulpicia,
but my Latin was very shaky.
She said she didn't know why I would need any.

*So you won't be able to comment
on the recently found fragments
which are being attributed to her?*

I could have a shot, but my Latin has vast holes in it.

*Look this is only a short piece,
do you think you could wing it for a few minutes
with a bit of padding and repetition?*

But I don't want to look foolish,
I have my reputation to protect.

*Yes, yes. We'll double your fee to seventy pounds,
and invite you back as our authority on poetry...
when we need one.*

That would be ideal.
Let's talk about her passionate love affair,
I'm good at passion.

Being Consoled by Oscar

Hello matey. Down boy, stop jumping about.
I bombed tonight, saw a bloke's chin drop
on his chest and he wasn't even asleep.

I read a new poem, wanted to give it a test run.
It got a very muted response, must work out why.
Maybe it's just a rotten poem. Perhaps it was

too blatant, some prefer a bit of subtlety.
I think I'll leave it a few days, even a week
or a few months, see how I feel. Mind you,

it might be the audience wasn't listening,
I read near the end and it was a very long
evening and no one else was particularly

well received. I think I'll cut the reference
to swanky bankers, maybe it's a bit rude.
Hold on, perhaps it's not rude enough.

Thanks for the lick Oscar, I knew you'd agree.

Frank Asks George to Judge
a Poetry Competition

You'd be the sole judge, George. There should
be at least a thousand poems. Will you do it?

The trouble is, I'd tend to discard
all those highly polished poems,
especially if I prefer what's being said
over how it's written.

Yes, that could be a problem. Couldn't you be more
open to technically good work as well?

I'm not sure. It's how I'm wired. I'll accept
some flaws if I like the poem.

We could afford to pay you a nice cheque.

But I'm not that well-known.

Don't be modest. We think your name
will pull in the punters. What about if I asked
the lovely Sybil Archer to co-judge with you?
It could be fun.

Er, I've just remembered, I'm taking Mary
to the Isle of Wight around then. No offence to Sybil.
I would have loved to have judged with her.

Breakfast with Mary

You were late in last night.

My students can be quite demanding.

Oh? In what way?

Is there any porridge?

You finished it yesterday.

They want advice on poems after class.

So why do you agree?

The college wants students to complete
tutor satisfaction forms. This puts us
under a lot of pressure.

*George, can you tell me why you've only
got two pairs of Y-fronts left?*

I can't, dear. But I assure you,
I've never had to leave anywhere in a hurry.

Considering the Olympics at the Pub

George, did you apply for any tickets?

No I didn't. I can't bear huge, pushing
crowds. I'm only used to venues
with attendances of between five and fifty.
But Frank's got two tickets for something
called beach volleyball. He says I can come along.

That sounds a bit low key.

Frank says imagine a sunny day, rippling
sand on Horse Guards Parade and young
women bouncing about... then at lunchtime
a gander round St James's Park, feed the ducks
and find a place that does steak and kidney pie.
Frank says lunch is my responsibility.

It seems Frank has thought of everything.

Just as well, I can't be trusted.

*But how do you know women
will be playing when you go?*

I asked Frank and he said I must have faith.

The Poetry Critic

I'm George Meadows. You weren't very generous
about my last book. In fact you verged
on the rude. Didn't you understand the poems?

Oh, there was something to understand, was there?

There you go again. Were you born rude
or is it an affectation?

I don't have to stand here and listen to this.

Where would you rather go then?

I'll see you're never reviewed again.

I suppose you're just one of those people
who can't do it, so they review it.
Wasn't there anything you liked about my work?

*Actually, I was rather taken with the way you write
about wine, use the grape as a metaphor for love
and passion. Like me, you know your wine.*

Yes, this is true. You wouldn't care
to share a bottle, would you?

I thought we were enemies.

Oh I don't think so. That's all forgotten,
especially since you'll be buying.

Having a One-to-One with a Student

Can we have a session on form, please?
The course outline did mention it.

What kind of form did you have in mind, Matilda –
bodily or racing?

You are funny, George. I mean poetry forms of course.
You know – sonnets, sestinas, villanelles.

Are you sure you really want to?
We don't want anyone becoming addicted, do we?

But it's not like drinking.

Oh no, it's not like drinking – I wish it were.
Take sonnets, achieving the end rhyme.
That can be addictive, especially if you're good at it.
Then add in the iambic beat and you'll soon
be obsessed with the little bugger. I'm sorry,
I shouldn't have used that language.

That's quite alright, but I don't think
sonnets sound at all pleasant. I don't want
to become an addict at my age.

I'm sure you've made the right decision.
In fact, I think I should have a word
with Health and Safety; we don't want
to encourage dependency.

George, Frank and Facebook

Now you're getting nominated for important prizes
you really should consider having a page on Facebook.

Not you as well, Frank. I couldn't bear all that gossip,
being talked about somewhere in the ether.

But you're being talked about already.

Yes, but I don't want to join in. I'm the first to say
I like a good gossip, but I prefer it with real
people, who I can see and hear –
down the pub or at a poetry gathering.
I know you've never put me wrong,
but I get along very nicely with my answer machine.

Ok, I understand. I only wanted to help.

I know and thank you. Let's go for a curry.
It's my turn to rubbish your poems.

Reading to Oscar

I've bought you a tin of your special –
get down, be patient, let me open it.

Hold on, I'm going to give you another
treat. How about a taste of beer?

Let me pour you a slurp or two.
It's London Pride. My favourite.

Now please settle down, I want to read you
my new sestina. Yes, I know that means

turning the page, but you'll find it soothing
so just be calm. This is good for you.

No it won't go on too long.

Being Commissioned to Write a Poem

Look at this, Oscar, I've been invited to write a poem
on 'space'. I'm lucky, I've already written two

on that subject. Stop that, I've told you it's rude.
The psychoanalysts asked me to write about 'inner space'.

That took me a long time, I had no idea about inner
space, it sounded a bit hocus-pocus. I came up

with a poem, but I didn't understand what I'd written.
They said it was just what they were hoping for –

something revealing about the inner self. Then
the aerospace boys asked me to write a poem

on 'outer space'. That was easy. I swatted up by
digging out my old Eagle comics. They were really

pleased, even praised my innocent and joyful
approach to the world. Anyway, I propose to take

the best lines from each and fuse them together into
a cohesive whole. No one will see the joins. I'll steer

the narrative towards 'personal space'. Most readers
will empathise with that. Even you, Oscar, like a bit

of peace in your kennel and I adore personal space,
so the poem should turn out alright. With luck they'll

love it and pay me promptly – yes, don't worry,
I know you want a bone and some de-worming pills.

Trying to Think of an Epigraph

Frank, I think this poem could do with an epigraph,
something to give it a bit of self-importance...
you know, elevation. Perhaps when I find one
I could get it translated into German –

that will enable me to explain at readings
it's from an early play by Brecht.
Of course, it isn't, but no one will know
and they will think I'm very clever.

Why are you shaking your head, Frank?

At the Newsagent

Why do you always come in on Saturdays, look through
The Guardian and New Statesman, then buy The Telegraph?

I'm sorry, it's become a bit of a habit.
I like reading the poems and seeing who's written them.
You're very indulgent, thank you.

But why do you then buy The Telegraph?

I enjoy the arts pages
and my wife says it's got a good travel section.

Do you travel a lot?

Thankfully not. Buying The Telegraph seems to do the trick.

Mysteriousness and Mary

Mary dear, I've had a letter from one of my readers.
The only one, I suspect. She asks why I don't have

mystery in my poems. She's studied all my books
and says it would add texture to my writing.

Perhaps I should be a bit ambiguous, leave
the poem hanging on the washing line's obscurity,

a plain sheet, flapping against a frilly pillow case.
Mary, would you like me to be more mysterious?

Or do you like having what you see?

Lunch with Cyril

Nice of you to buy, Cyril. Perhaps
you're making money out of me at last?

It's only a pub lunch, but as ever George,
you're perceptive when it comes to money.

Does that mean I'm going to get an advance
for the next book? I'd have to refuse.
I don't want to put myself under any pressure
earning it back for you.

No, we won't change any of our usual habits.

So why lunch?

I'm retiring. I want to take it easier.

If you take it much easier, Cyril,
you'll fall off your stool.
What's the real problem?
Nothing to do with plumbing, is it?
Take Frank, he's off to the loo after just one pint.

George, please listen. I'm getting married.

What, at your age? Who's the lucky lady?

It's Sybil.

Sybil! I'm losing you to Sybil?
What about our nights out? She'll stop that,
she's very suburban, insists on dusting every day.
You don't know her very well.
Why don't you opt for a long, a very long engagement,
hope her memory packs in before yours?

Discussing his New
Collection with Cyril

Thanks for coming in, George.
It's very good –
but rather different from your usual stuff.

Yes, I've tried to be brave,
there might not be another one.

You always say that.

I feel different this time.
Did you like everything?

As always you're brilliant most of the time,
but I won't let anything through
which lets you down, or me.

That's what I like about you, Cyril,
 you get your cuffs dirty.

Yes George, very dirty.

And it's most appreciated. We've known
each other a long time, started
on the same day. We were nineteen, trying
to think up slogans in a fug of fag smoke.
Do you remember the secretaries?
I've given up smoking now.
Aren't I a good boy?

I wouldn't say that, George.

By the way, how's dear Sybil,
is she keeping the flat clean?
Does she let you smoke at home?

The Queen Elizabeth Hall

Don't worry old chum, I'm not going
to leave you, The Queen Elizabeth Hall

can wait. It might have been nice, a twenty-
minute reading, and all the audience staring

back at me – that's if anyone turned up.
You wouldn't have known who to bark at first.

They said they couldn't find you a billet.
I was tempted to smuggle you in, just me

and you Oscar, on stage. That's what I call
fun. They didn't understand we're mates.

Frank-the-fixer has gone on instead. He's
persuaded them to ask me again. Easy boy,

I'm taking you to the quack tomorrow. He'll
give you something to make you comfortable.

At the Vet with Oscar

Bob, can you sort the old boy out?
He seems a bit off.

Let's have him up here. That's better.
Yes, he doesn't seem his usual
disreputable self...
have you felt this in his groin?

No, I haven't. Perhaps I should have brought
him in earlier. Oh dear, I didn't notice.

Don't beat yourself too hard. They appear
from nowhere.

Can we do anything?

Not really.

Ah, I see.
Can I give him one last request?
Let me take him for a walk
back home through the park,
a sniff at the new daffodils.

Then tomorrow morning, first call,
could you come round... and see him off?
He's been sleeping a lot.
He'll be in his basket.
I'll put my old dressing gown round him.

Waiting for the Wine

Good, here it comes, the wine again.
'Just a bit more. That's generous, thank you.'

Why's he buying five anthologies?
He's only got a haiku in it.

With a bit of luck it'll sell out
and I won't have to buy a copy.

'Yes, thanks, just a half-glass.
Are there any olives?'

Good God, I thought he was dead,
he should be, he looks very pasty.

'What? No, I can't stay for the readings.
No, I'm not in the book. Missed the deadline.'

Ah, that's why she gave him a good review...
'Yes thanks, just a drop more, oops –

No, don't worry, I'll wipe it off.'
There really should have been some nibbles.

Oh-oh, the old bore's spotted me.
'Excuse me, must sit down. Get the weight off.'

That's better. 'More? Alright, thanks.'
Lovely wine, dry and crisp. Just

one more, then I'll be gone.

With the Doctor

I've known you twenty years, doctor.
May I call you by your first name?
I've been feeling a bit dodgy,

tell it to me straight, you know,
just clear, unambiguously,
I don't have a Latin dictionary.

Is it serious... Mervyn? Go on
just say it, I'm not going to faint...
No, not much at all, it's definitely

just social drinking. Yes,
it's always been that.
Thanks for being straight, doctor.

I'll see you in three months. I'm glad
it's nothing serious. By the way,
what's the name of that pretty

receptionist? Oh, she's your wife.
Yes, I'm going.

With Mary after a College Reading

How did it go dear? Were you appreciated?

It depends on what you mean by appreciated.

You know what I mean.

I thought I read well, but some students lack
respect, even started to talk... more disturbing,
I'm still getting showered with poems to advise on.

This appointment seems to be wearing you out.

It is. Also, my own creativity has suffered.
It's as if I don't own myself any more.
What's that thick envelope on my desk?

It was wedged in the letter box when I came in.

You know what it is, don't you?

Yes dear, let me send it back.
Let's watch that Flog It you recorded.

No thank you, I'm going to bed.

George is Run Out

I'm awake. Don't hover Mary, come in.
I feel a bit short of breath, as if a long ball

has been thrown in from the boundary
and I've been run out.

I've told Frank what I want.
He's been given enough to make sure...

Blow me a kiss –
please turn on Newsnight.
I'm a bit drowsy...

At his Own Funeral

The view is perfect, like being in the dress circle
of a small theatre, but facing the audience. I'm
sorry for Mary and the kids. That's the worst thing

about dying, you see all the upset. What the hell's
he doing here? He always gave me a bad review,
never even bought me a pint. Oh, there's Sybil.

I enjoyed her rejections, even the ones which weren't
for my poetry. Or did I reject her? I gave instructions
for plenty of wine, I hope to glug a few glasses. Damn,

I forgot I'm dead. I've seen all those I love. Nearly
everyone has been very generous, but that old fart,
what's his name, he was a rude bugger. I've never

been drunk in public, hardly ever. I'm quite proud of that.
And the old girl with the half-open blouse, she was all
tittle-tattle. I didn't try it on, at least I don't think I did.

Must be her imagination. Well, it's nearly over.
Poetry has been fun, but as Frank said,
I never won a big one. Do I care? I bloody well do.

Hold on... is that Oscar barking?

George Hopes for Post-Death Glory

The Telegraph wrote the best piece; it strayed
into two columns, quoted some good lines,
said I added character to the literary scene.
I can live with that... except I'm dead.
The photo had me holding a full glass,
in shorts with my beaten-up panama

and sideways grin. Even The Guardian
found space for some coded compliments.
The local press wrote a sympathetic couple
of paragraphs. They seemed to have forgotten
the torrent of correspondence, our little tiff.

My poetry pals from the Morning After Club
are thinking of a memorial dinner at an Italian
in Soho, lots of pasta, fried courgettes and Chianti.
That'll remind me of the good old nights

when I often slept on the floor –
don't ask who with. I'd like to see Gavin again.
I've missed him. He was marvellously salacious.

Oh dear, I wonder if I'll like being dead...
That was Oscar barking. Where is he?

Trust him to have the last word.

Letter to a Literary Editor

There's been much correspondence
about the late George Meadows.
I use the word ' late' advisedly,
as many of your readers know
he was always late, but apologized
with such a charming smile

it was difficult not to forgive him
or buy the first round of drinks.
In response to Professor Baxter's letter,
that George was often gratuitous,
I would say he perfected
the art of gratuitousness.

Even Ted Hughes admired his work,
particularly the much anthologised poem
'Latrines'. He wrote to George, saying
he saw a much deeper meaning
and understood it was really about

the urge of the human condition.
This pleased George a lot.
He felt that if he ever had the pleasure
of standing, head bowed, next to Ted
in the Gents, he would remind him of this
but hoped his remarks

would not be misinterpreted,
since he and Ted had never
been introduced. Finally,
I want to correct the impression
that George drank himself to death.
This is completely wrong. We shared

a doctor, who told me George's liver function
was perfectly normal for a man of his age.
Also, George was thinking of leaving
his body for research, but unfortunately
never got round to it.

We will have to be satisfied with his poems.

Cyril Bunion, Bunion Press

George's last poem found after his death

Last Night
(for M)

Last night you smiled a lot
said *Tonight is for us.*

And when I poured the wine,
lifted my glass and drank,
it was as if you kissed me,
not on the lips, but inside.

I watched you toss the salad;
can still see the patchwork of lettuce
flopping back into the bowl
as dressing sprayed the air.

Then you placed some on my plate
and I returned the olives,
lifted my glass,
felt you kiss me again.

During the meal we talked a little,
but not too much.

I ate a kind of peace last night.

George's very last poem found in a shoe

Love Poem in a Shoe

I want you in feet, chains and furlongs,
I need you all day long.
I'd love to take you incognito,
naked now, in red stilettos.

About the Author

Peter Phillips is a London poet. His last collection,
No School Tie, was released by Ward Wood Publishing
in 2011.

His three previous collections, all published by Hearing Eye,
were:

Wide Skies, Salt and Best Bitter, 2005
Looking For You, 2001
Frayed At The Edges (pamphlet), 1997

For more about this author online see his pages:
on the *poetry pf* website www.poetrypf.co.uk
and on www.wardwoodpublishing.co.uk